MW01137603

NEVER ENDING WONDERS

NEVER ENDING WONDERS

Inspired Acronyms to Shift Your
Perspective and Open Your Heart

JJ CROW

WORLDCHANGERS MEDIA

Paperback: 978-1-955811-58-3
E-book: 978-1-955811-59-0
LCCN: 2023922632

First paperback edition: January 2024

Edited by Bryna Haynes / www.WorldChangers.media

Published by WorldChangers Media
PO Box 83, Foster, RI 02825
www.WorldChangers.Media

DEDICATION

This book is dedicated to Jay Chambers and all of the other truth seekers who encouraged me to create a book of my "Acrownyms," and who donated time and money to make it happen.
Thank you.

TABLE OF CONTENTS

A.C.R.O.W.N.Y.M.S.

A Clear Revelation Of Wisdom Now
Yielding Meaningful Support

Hello! My name is JJ Crow, aka "Gamma."

Messages from my higher power began coming to me spontaneously in the form of acronyms over thirty years ago. I usually received them when I was walking in nature. These acronyms were new definitions of common words and phrases, and usually provided a much-needed shift in perspective around whatever was on my mind at the time.

I enjoyed sharing the wisdom these acronyms imparted with family and friends. They would thank me for sharing, then write them down for later reference. I started doing the same.

I knew that the wisdom being given to me was a unique gift from Spirit to assist me in my evolution. I began calling them "A-crow-nyms," a play on my last name. They came so often I created newsletters to share them, along with stories of how they assisted me. I received a lot of gratitude and encouragement to create a book of them. You are holding the result of that encouragement in your hands right now!

How to Use This Book

Using the Acrownyms can help you quickly shift from stressful doing to peaceful being. Taking the hero's journey of self-inquiry leads us to our joyful selves. It empowers us with supernatural gifts of healing and manifestation.

The most powerful way to use this book is to choose an Acrownym each morning and meditate on it as you walk in nature or sit in stillness. You can work through the book in order, or open to a random page and let Spirit guide you to the message you need each day. (I prefer the second approach, since Spirit always knows what we need to continue to grow and shift!)

If you are struggling with a particular challenge in your life, you can also find the Acrownyms that speak to you and work with those until a new, more joyful energy emerges inside you. Sometimes, all it takes is a small reframing of a well-known concept to completely shift your perspective.

I encourage you to be a trailblazer. To follow your inner guidance every step of the way. To find your own unique creative expression. Your courage will lead you to a more youthful, abundant and vibrant life.

With love and joy,

Gamma

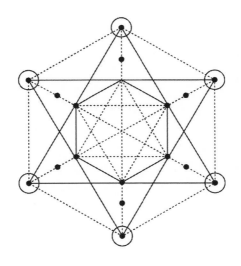

THE "ACROWNYMS"

A.B.U.N.D.A.N.C.E.

**A Beautiful Unlimited New Dance
Allowing Natural Creative Expression**

Doing what I love and loving what I do inspires
authentic creative expression. Expressing myself
without needing anyone's permission or approval
feels like dancing with abandon. It feels heavenly.

B.L.I.S.S. #1

Being Loving Is So Satisfying

One day, I was out walking when I felt orgasmic love
flowing through me. It was the love of my divine female
and male energy in balance. I didn't need anything
outside of myself to complete me. Feeling whole is bliss.

BL.I.S.S. #2

Being Loved Is So Sweet

Until I learned to love myself, I didn't feel I deserved
to be loved by others. My relationships changed when I
experienced the female/male divine balance within myself.
Then, I was able to relate to the essence within everyone,
not the false self they were projecting. People respond with
love and gratitude when they are seen as their true selves.

C.A.L.M.

Conscious Actions Living Mindfully

I take deep breaths and slow down when I feel
confused or anxious. This relaxes my mind and
body. Then, I listen to my heart for guidance. I know
what to do next when I am calm and relaxed.

C.H.O.I.C.E.

**Constantly Honoring Ourselves
Is Clearly Empowering**

I do what is right for me when I choose to listen to my
heart. What other people think, or what they choose
to do about my choices, doesn't concern me. I know
what is right for me is right for everyone. This has been
one of the most liberating realizations of my life.

C.O.O.L.

Conscious Of Our Light

I have the awareness that I am an integral part
of creation's unity. Feeling separate causes pain
and anxiety. Nothing can separate me from the
wholeness I am and feel. That is definitely cool!

CO.L.O.R.

Can Our Love Overcome Repression?

Love cannot be repressed. It is the creative force of
the universe. I overcome repression by loving myself
and aligning with the frequency of love. Yes, we can
overcome repression. It is our power of choice!

D.A.N.C.E.

Divinity And Nature Creating Ecstasy

Nature flows endlessly without expectations. It
simply expresses Itself. My heart overflows with joy
when I align with life's natural rhythm. I listen to
the birds. I smell the flowers. I watch the sunrises
and sunsets. I am in awe of the moon and stars. Life
is an ecstatic dance I like to join and enjoy!

E.N.D.

Energy Never Dies

Nothing dies. Everything is continuously changing form. I am infinite, forever evolving. Knowing this gives me peace of mind. Death does not frighten me. I do not worry about how long it will take to fulfill my dreams. I am present with whatever I am doing. I know now is all there ever is. I fully enjoy this moment!

F.A.I.T.H. #1

Finding Answers In The Heart

I stop and meditate when I am seeking answers.
My consciousness expands. I am receptive to guidance.
My heart is the captain of my ship, my mind is my assistant.
There is smooth sailing when I let my heart lead.

F.A.I.T.H. #2

Freedom Actually Is Truth Happening

Being courageous strengthened my faith muscle.
Since everything is always happening for the best, I
fearlessly embrace the unknown. I release fear quickly
when it arises. I developed a strong faith muscle by
facing my fears and acting courageously over and over
again. Unwavering faith leads to everlasting joy.

F.A.I.T.H. #3

Finding Acceptance Is The Hurdle

Understanding the meaning of this one was the beginning of me accepting whatever happens and learning from the experience. I realized that wanting something to go my way was assuming my mind knew better than my heart. How absurd is that?

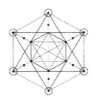

F.E.A.R.

Forgetting Everything's Already Right

I trust that everything is happening for the best, so
I shift my awareness from my dark thoughts to my
heart's knowing. The universe is a harmonious unit
of pure consciousness. I know better than to want
it to conform to my mundane expectations.

G.A.M.M.A.

Grace And Myself Magically Aligned

My grandson, Anthony, has called me Gamma
since he could speak. Gamma rays are the highest
frequencies. That is where the wisdom and truth I share
comes from. I meditate and align with these higher
frequencies where I experience wisdom and joy.

G.L.A.D.

Gratitude Lightens And Delights

Gratitude lifts me from the ordinary into the infinite.
It is infectious. I sincerely care about others.
I ask others about their lives. That is what I do at the
grocery store, library, farmer's market or wherever
I am. It is fun to see people's frowns turn into
smiles. Their light warms my heart. Our encounters
become mutually rewarding exchanges.

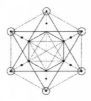

G.O.D.

Go On Dancing

This Acrownym is the perfect description of higher consciousness. Moving harmoniously with the rhythms of Nature is the dance of life. Most cultures dance to connect with their souls. Let's dance!

G.R.A.C.E.

Goodness Resonates As Compassionate Expression

Everyone acts out negatively because of past conditioning.
My behavior is less than ideal when I am triggered.
I forgive myself for my human actions, and I forgive
other's behavior with compassion.
Grace is loving unconditionally.

G.U.I.L.T.Y.

Giving Unnecessary Insult Lethal To Yourself

When I act or speak unconsciously, and realize I have behaved incorrectly, I ask for forgiveness. I do what I can to rectify the situation. Then, I forgive myself. To keep feeling guilty creates disharmony in the body and mind. It is harmful and serves no useful purpose.

H.A.P.P.Y. #1

Harmony And Play Prosper You

"You never work a day in your life when you are doing what you love." This is a truism. I actually find being playful gives me energy and fills me with joy. Creating from that place is my definition of prosperity.

H.A.P.P.Y. #2

Happiness and Peace Promote Youthfulness

The more I am in harmony with myself, the younger I feel. Happiness heals organically without drugs or diets. I express love to every cell, every system, and every part of my body every day. My body responds by giving me more enthusiastic, creative energy. This is my anti-aging formula.

H.E.A.V.E.N.

Honoring Existence And Valuing Everything Now

I live in heaven on earth. Heaven is a state of mind.
It is not a place to find elsewhere. When I realized
that I am pure love, and so is everyone else, my
life became an ongoing heavenly adventure.

H.E.L.L.

Hearts Experiencing Lacking Love

Separation from love is the only sin. I separate
myself from love when I let my thoughts control
my life. I rise from the terror of hell when I listen
to my heart, the home of unconditional love.

H.E.L.L.O.

Hearts Experiencing Love Lift Others

People know when they are in the presence of love.
Love glows. I walk most days on the bike path. Meeting
people and having a moment of sharing is delightful.
Some people are not open to saying hello. My loving
heart communicates to their hearts anyway. The
vibration of love penetrates all things, everywhere.

H.I.

Hearts Interacting

My heart is continuously interacting with all
life. That's why I stay present and communicate
unconditional love wherever I am.

I.F.

Intellectual Fantasy

When this Acrownym came to me, I couldn't stop laughing. I used to imagine negative outcomes and feel anxious about many things. I began shifting my imagination to beneficial outcomes, especially when things seemed to be otherwise. This practice has changed my relationships, my self-awareness, and my outlook. My whole life is better now.

J.O.Y.

Just Open Yourself

Love is all there is. I stay open and allow it to fill my heart. I read somewhere, "Open yourself and relax." How easy is that? Yet, we make everything so complicated until we learn to let ourselves be guided, comforted, and sustained. Then, being joyful is natural.

J.O.Y.F.U.L.

Just Open Yourself For Unconditional Love

Shifting from my thoughts to the silence within opens
the channel for unconditional love to flow through
me. Then, my heart naturally overflows with joy and
gratitude. I feel love wherever I am, whatever I am
doing. Be anchored in the joyful frequency of love.

K.E.Y.

Knowledge Enlightens You

Enlightenment is the reward of self-understanding.
"Know thyself and the truth will set you free." Taking the
courageous hero's journey into self-awareness is the key
that unlocks the door to freedom and a blissful life.

L.A.U.G.H.

Love And Uninhibited Gladness Heal

My joyful inner companion entertains me with wise
downloads. I laugh out loud with joy when the truth is
revealed to me in new Acrownyms. They liberate me from
the self-imposed prison of negative thoughts. I laugh
often, even when I am alone. Laughter is truly healing.

L.A.W.

Love And Wisdom

Man's law is to regulate behavior and punish those who do not conform. Love is self-regulating. My heart's wisdom is the natural law of unconditional love for myself and all life.

L.E.T.T.I.N.G. G.O.

**Love Eliminates Troubled Thinking Invoking
Natural Genius Giving Opulence**

I let go of my human perspective. I let fear, worry, doubt
and my personal wishes go. Life brings forth inspiration
and truth when I let go. I allow grace to happen through
me. Then, opulent gifts are transmitted to me.

L.I.S.T.E.N.

Letting Intuitive Self-Truth Enter Naturally

This is the gift that changed my life. I realized I had to be still and listen for the truth to be revealed. I started keeping the channels open for guidance to enlighten me wherever I was or whatever I was doing. When I notice I am distracted, I get quiet within. Truth flows continuously when I listen.

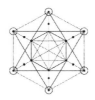

L.O.O.K.

Love Observes Our Kinship

Humans have the same desires and challenges everywhere. Natural disasters and covid made it very clear that we are part of a global family. I look at the world and others through my divine lens. This outlook gives me happiness and peace. I pray for grace for all of my brothers and sisters equally.

L.O.S.T.

Lacking One's Self-Truth

I was lost. My conditioned lack of self-esteem mislead me.
Out of fear I made decisions that sabotaged me. I attracted
dysfunctional relationships. I hurt the ones I loved. Despair
created pain in my mind, illness in my body and prevented
me from achieving my goals. I was lost until I listened
to my heart for answers and made healthy choices.

L.O.V.E.

Letting Ourselves Value Everyone

We have all heard, "Judge not least you be judged." I discovered that whatever I judge in another person is something I despise in myself. That was a rude awakening. I was critical of others when my thoughts and actions were unconscious. What I saw in others was a reflection of my own misguided thoughts and behavior. Loving myself allows me to value everyone's unique journey.

M.A.J.E.S.T.I.C.

**My Actions Joyously Express Soul's
True Inner Connection**

I acknowledge my sovereignty. "I honor my own inner
self" is the meaning of the Hindu mantra, *Om Namah
Shivaya*. Self-empowerment is knowing that no one
has power over me unless I relinquish my power.

M.A.G.I.C.

Mystery And Grace In Cahoots

The mysteries of life can only be known by revelation. Truth is revealed to me when I am in a state of grace, surrendered to the unknown. The powers greater than myself are in cahoots to liberate me. This is magic.

M.A.N.I.F.E.S.T.

**My Actions Now Increase Frequency
Evoking Supreme Treasures**

Living spontaneously is the act of surrendering to a
power greater than myself. I trust my higher Self to
guide my steps. I let go so that what I need is provided
effortlessly. What is necessary to fulfill my desires manifests
supremely at the right time, and in the right way.

M.A.R.R.I.A.G.E.

Mutual Appreciation Richly Rewards
Individuals Allowing Greater Exchanges

Each partner loving themselves and respecting the
sovereignty of the other makes a rewarding marriage.
My interactions with people are mutually reciprocal
now that I love and respect myself and others.

M.I.R.A.C.L.E.

Magic Is Really A Contagious Loving Experience

Love created me. Love nurtures me. Love sustains me.
Love heals me. Love comforts me. Love is contagious. The
more I love, the more I am loved. Miracles are natural.

M.O.N.E.Y. #1

My Obsessions Never Ease Yearnings

Get one thing, want more, get the next thing, want more. Discontentment with what I had caused disappointment and depression. I realized that no amount of money would every be enough. There would always be something else to desire.

M.O.N.E.Y. #2

Making Our Natural Energy Yield

Money is just energy. I accumulate abundance by using my creative energy. Positive energy attracts positive energy. What I give I receive. The more grateful I am, the more I have to be grateful for. I am content with what I have. Contentment is priceless.

M.O.T.H.E.R.

Mother's Open Tender Heart Embraces Relations

My heart overflows when I remember how my mother would tenderly spoon me when I was ill. Her holding me lovingly is a feeling I will always cherish. My mother used to say, "If you can't say something nice about a person, don't say anything at all." She was always kind. Her sweet example helped me be a loving person.

M.Y.S.T.I.C.

Mind Yields So Truth Is Communicated

I let my mind rest so I can hear what my soul is
communicating. My mind thinks, my soul knows.
Aligning my body, mind, and soul empowers
me to share wisdom with others. Each step is
guided when I surrender to Self-awareness.

N.E.W.

Never Ending Wonders

Everything is new every moment. Being aware of this makes my life an ongoing adventure. I wake up childlike and excited about what my day will bring. I actually love not knowing what will happen next. I know what needs to happen will happen in the right way, and at the right time.

N.O.W.

No Other Way

Meditation, for me, is being present with whatever I am doing, right here, right now. My mind lives in the past or the future. My past has taught me valuable lessons. What I do now will determine my future. I imagine the things I want to do and have while enjoying this moment now. This is a way to Self-enlightenment.

O.N.E.

Our Natural Essence

Scientists have proven that everything in existence is
interconnected and interdependent. When I harm myself,
I harm everyone and everything. When I honor myself,
I honor all life. This knowledge makes me cognizant
of my responsibility. I want my thoughts, words, and
actions to impact all that is in a harmonious way.

O.P.E.N.

One's Potential Expands Now

Keeping my heart open allows inner guidance to take charge. Nothing can limit me except my own limiting thoughts. I choose to stay open for infinite possibilities to manifest. That is why my life is magical and full of grace.

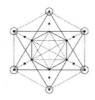

O.U.T.C.O.M.E.

One's Uninhibited Trust Creates Opulent Manifestations Effortlessly

I imagine my body being healthy. I imagine my wealth
increasing exponentially. I imagine my creations being
life-changing tools that inspire and uplift humanity.
I imagine life being creative, fulfilling, and joyful.
And that is the life I live every day, every moment.

P.L.A.Y.

Peace, Love And Youthfulness

Being childlike with a peaceful mind keeps me forever
young at heart. I love everything I am doing when I
am doing it. Letting spirit flow through me to create
inspiring tools is pure joy. Being in the flow is fun,
beneficial, and rewarding beyond my imagination.

P.O.O.R.

Personality Obstructing Own Resources

My thoughts and words sabotaged my inner resources.
I was poor until I journeyed within and discovered my
unlimited, eternal, unique self. My thoughts and words are
self-respecting, positive, and loving now. I am poor no more!

P.O.S.I.T.I.V.E.

**Power Of Soul Instinctively Trusting
Its Victorious Existence**

Trusting my inner nature is the positive act that
keeps my body, mind, and spirit in coherence.
Victorious outcomes result when existing in
coherence with myself and all of creation.

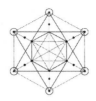

P.O.W.E.R.

Personality One With Eternal Rhythm

My personal power comes from surrendering my human
personality to higher consciousness. I flow with the
rhythm of the universe. This power cannot be repressed.
It is sovereign. It is truthful and fearless. It is everlasting.

P.R.A.I.S.E.

Pure Reverence Acknowledging
Infinite Source Energy

Giving thanks for the infinite miracle that is life is a
practice that attracts more miracles. I throw up my
arms in praise often during the day, even when I am
out walking. I don't need to keep a gratitude journal
because I say, "Thank You, Lord!" all day long.

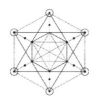

P.R.E.S.E.N.C.E.

Powerful Radiance Enveloping Soul's
Essence Now Causes Enlightenment

I feel the powerful radiance embracing me when I stay present. I feel my soul's expansive nature when I am still. I am aware I am more than my physical mind and body. My path is divinely guided. My purpose is clear.

P.R.I.C.E.L.E.S.S.

**Person Resourceful In Creative Expression
Lives Easily Sustaining Success**

My success does not depend on anything outside
of myself. I am successful, because I know who I
am. I am successful, because I do what I love. I am
successful, because my creative expression brings
me happiness. Self-empowerment is priceless.

P.R.I.S.O.N.

Person Rejecting Intuition Suffering
Oppression Needlessly

I was in a prison of my own making when I let my false
beliefs and conditioning run my life. Negative thoughts
kept me in prison needlessly until I had the courage
to face my demons and choose my thoughts. A person
in prison can actually be free, sovereign, and at peace
in their heart and mind. Self-awareness liberates.

P.U.R.P.O.S.E. #1

Perfect Understanding Reaps Powerful
Opportunities Supporting Evolution

My purpose is to share my gifts that elevate awareness.
Source energy supports those who seek wisdom
with powerful opportunities that prosper.

P.U.R.P.O.S.E. #2

Person Understanding Right Priorities
Offer Satisfying Experiences

Putting my Creator first and letting integrity lead is a
blissful experience. Being in the creative zone is the most
satisfying feeling there is. It is fulfilling and often orgasmic.

Q.U.E.S.T.

Quietly Unfolding Essential Self-Truth

My evolution provides true wisdom, raises my frequency, and increases my skills. I am a "PHD," Person Happily Developing. My quest is to embody truth and wisdom.

Q.U.I.E.T.L.Y.

Quantum Understanding Is
Eternal Truth Liberating You

I know that I am part of All That Is. I belong. I matter. This awareness makes me feel expansive and unlimited. It allows me to explore new horizons.

R.A.D.I.A.N.T.

Receiving A Divine Initiation And
Naturally Transcending

The earth, and all of creation, is being showered with
more Light than ever before. Wisdom that used to
be for the few chosen ones is now freely available to
anyone who opens their heart. Transcending the human
conditioning and living free is my natural birthright.
I embrace what is true and eternal. I radiate joy!

R.A.P.T.U.R.E.

**Realizing And Practicing Truth
Unceasingly Releases Ecstasy**

I say, "Thank you. I love you," to all the cells, systems, organs, glands, etc., in my body every day. I appreciate that my body is the greatest miracle in existence. My body responds in ecstasy. It is tuned in, turned on, and transcended. I feel tantric love all by myself.

R.E.A.L.

Recognizing Everything As Love

Everyone is pure love at heart. We move from our loving,
knowing essence into feeling separate. This distorts
our senses and affects our judgment. One day, I saw a
peculiar-looking man and was critical in my mind. Then
I realized that his appearance didn't matter. I smiled
and thought, "Love is really dressed up funny today."

R.E.A.L.L.Y.

Recognizing Everything As Love Liberates You

Love liberates me moment to moment. When my
mind starts to find fault with others, or I feel less
than whole, I pause and remember that everything
is Love. My heart overflows with gratitude. This
gratitude returns me to my pure, loving essence.

R.E.C.E.I.V.E.

Receptive Energy Connects Everything
Imparting Victorious Experiences

I live in a state of grace. My connection to everything
I want already exists. One of my favorite teachings
is, "Open to receive and rest." What is meant for my
evolution comes to me naturally, because I am open and
receiving. That is the beauty of surrendering. It is grace.

R.E.J.O.I.C.E.

**Reverently Expressing Joy Openly
Is Communicating Ecstasy**

I give thanks for my blessings often. I feel an intimate
connection with everything around me. I hug trees
every day on my walks. My heart sings when I hear
bird songs. Butterflies dancing delight me. An
open, grateful heart makes rejoicing natural.

R.E.L.I.E.F.

Releasing Emotions Lets Inner Essence Flow

I used to be afraid to express my emotions. I didn't set boundaries. Conflict terrified me. I had no voice. Then I learned to acknowledge my feelings. Now I express my feelings without judging myself. It is a relief to allow myself to be human. Awareness empowers me.

R.E.L.I.S.H.I.N.G.

Really Enjoying Life In Sweet
Harmony Is Now Gratifying

I relish the diverse gifts life offers. No two people of
billions are the same. I am fascinated by life's mysteries.
One can devote their entire life to learning about
one subject and still find new things to discover.
Life is an amazing, never-ending adventure.

R.E.S.I.L.I.E.N.T.

**Realizing Energy Simply Is Love
In Ever New Transition**

I am not fully present when my mind is thinking
about what I have to do next, or concerned about
something that may or may not happen in the future.
When I feel anxious, tired, or drained, I know to pause
and get centered. My energy quickly shifts back to
my loving, knowing self; present, here and now.

R.E.S.O.N.A.T.E.

**Responding Energy Sensing One's
Natural And True Existence**

It is rapturous to resonate with my own true nature.
With my inhale, I imagine being the ocean wave
caressing the shore. I pause. On my exhale, I am the
wave merging back into the ocean. I pause, then
repeat several times. This calms my nerves and relaxes
my body. My pulse resonates with creation.

R.E.S.P.E.C.T.

**Regard Each Soul's Purpose
Elevating Common Ties**

Shakespeare said, "All the world's a stage, and all men and women merely players." I know this to be the truth. I value each person's part. The good, the bad, and the ugly. It takes all kinds of characters to make a great play.

R.E.S.P.O.N.S.I.B.I.L.I.T.Y.

**Realize Each Stage Presents Opportunities
Necessary Since Improvement Brings Inner
Liberation Important To Yourself**

I take 100 percent responsibility for what happens in my
life. If I don't like what I am experiencing, I check within
to find out why I attracted it. What erroneous thoughts
or incorrect behavior caused the situation? I then have
the opportunity to make choices that attract experiences
I do want. This life is for learning and evolving.

R.E.S.T.

Relaxed Energy Silently Transforms

I stop to rest in silence when I am tired. My body relaxes and my mind gets clear. Rest is rejuvenating and healing. A little rest when needed transforms my experiences. I feel happy and ready to go again.

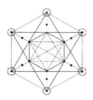

S.A.D.

Sorrowful And Disappointed

My life is not always a walk in the park. I have challenges.
I let myself feel the sadness and disappointment.
Then I release the energy to be transmuted. Sadness
lowers my frequency. Joy attracts positive changes.

S.A.T.I.S.F.I.E.D.

Staying Aligned To Infinite Soul Fulfills Individual's Ernest Desires

I stay satisfied by listening to my heart and following guidance. Satisfaction is actually a state of mind. It does not depend on one's circumstances. It is a choice.

S.E.C.U.R.E.

Surrendering Ego Creates Unequaled Rewarding Experiences

The ego has a valuable place. It carries out the desires of the heart. Insecurity is the result of letting the ego be in charge. Grace is the unequaled reward of letting the heart lead.

S.E.E.

Spirit Experiencing Existence

Existence is the result of Spirit wanting to experience Itself.
Contrast is what makes experiences interesting. Seeing
is not merely eyesight. Seeing is the awareness that life is
eternal Love having experiences in the human form.

S.E.E.K.I.N.G.

Self Embodying Eternal Knowledge
Is Now Gratified

I don't remember a time when I wasn't seeking
divine knowledge. Now, each revelation of awareness
gives me more wisdom. My mind is liberated. My
soul is supported, sustained, and comforted.

S.E.L.F.

Soul Expressing Love Forever

I am whole when my innate human wisdom merges with
my soul. My foremost intention is to keep this sacred
connection activated. That requires staying present, listening
to my heart, and letting love lead. Then, I am connected
to my miraculous Self, where all things are possible.

S.H.A.R.E.

Support Has A Rewarding Effect

I receive support from All That Is when I respect the gifts
life offers. Everything, including inanimate objects, wants
to be acknowledged. I thank water, fire, earth, and air for
sustaining me. I thank the sun, moon, and stars. I thank
all other species for the gifts they give unconditionally.

S.H.I.N.E.

Sparkling Heart Is Naturally Enthusiastic

People thank me for shinning my light. My enthusiasm
is contagious. This is the time for our natural
lights to shine brightly on whatever/whomever is
attempting to repress our creative self-awareness.
Love is always the answer. Right here, right now.

S.I.L.E.N.C.E.

Self Is Listening Emitting
Natural Calm Energy

"Be quiet and let me think," is often said when
one needs inner direction. Stilling my mind and
calming my body is unparalleled for hearing
answers that provide clarity and peace of mind.

S.I.M.P.L.E.

**Soul Is Manifesting
Pure Love's Essence**

My soul just loves. My mind thinks and confuses me
when I am thinking about the past or the future. I express
Love when I am present in my heart. It is that simple.

S.I.N.

Stuck In Negativity

When my mind is stuck in the past or future,
I lose clarity. Then I make unhealthy choices.
The only sin is separation from Love.

S.M.I.L.E.

Sharing My Inner Love Enthusiastically

Being centered, present, and loving is an ecstatic experience.
It cannot be contained. Everyone and everything I
see is Love in expression. I enthusiastically smile at
everyone because I recognize their true essence.

S.O.U.R.C.E.

Spirit's Opulent Unending Radiance
Creates Everything

My creative spirit is unlimited and effervescent.
My inspiration and guidance come to
me directly from Source energy.

S.P.A.R.K.L.E.S.

**Sincere Positive Awareness Radiating
Kindness Lifting Energy Significantly**

A woman on my walk spoke negatively. I tried changing the
subject to something pleasant, but she went on complaining.
I just kept seeing her as Love. It took a while, but now when
I see her she is smiling. She even shares positive quotes with
me. Love and kindness bring out the sparkle in people.

S.P.I.R.I.T.

Supreme Power Is Radiant Invincible Truth

"What is essential is invisible to the eye," is a quote from *The Little Prince* by Antoine de Saint-Exupery. Love, truth and wisdom are eternal—and the invincible radiance of creation.

S.T.A.R.L.I.G.H.T.

**Soul Transcends And Radiates Love
In Glittering Heart's Truth**

We come from the stars. I transcend my human
conditions and elevate my frequency to pure light.
That is why people are always telling me, "You are
glowing." Happy people glow, because they know
who they are. They know they are here to shine.

S.T.R.E.S.S.

Spending Time Rarely Experiencing
Self-Sensitivity

Doing, doing, doing without stopping to be is stressful.
It disturbs my mind. It makes me ill. I enjoy stopping
to feel what my body needs. I become refreshed and
energized. Then I know my next best action.

S.U.P.P.O.R.T.

Sharing Unconditionally Provides
Opulent Riches Today

I love the practice of "paying it forward" and doing things
for other people, especially when not asked. Giving
support freely, without expecting anything in return,
feels good. I see a need and fill it. My neighbors and I
willingly support each other. It is richly rewarding.

S.U.R.E.

Self-Understanding Richly Energizes

I absolutely trust my inner guidance to lead me
perfectly. Being sure leaves no space for doubt and
regret. Even when my choices lead to things I don't like
or want, I learn something I need for my growth.

S.U.R.R.E.N.D.E.R.

Self Unconditionally Releases Resistance
Engaging Natural Divine Eternal Resources

I quiet my mind's incessant chatter. I listen for divine
guidance. Universal intelligence shows me the way. I
have no worries. Grace is the reward of surrendering.

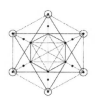

S.W.A.M.I.

Sacred Woman And Man Incarnate

This was the first Acrownym that came to me.
We all have male and female energy within.
Balancing my male and female energy creates sacred
coherence. Healing happens in the balance.

S.W.E.E.T.

Self Wisely Embraces Essential Truth

"How sweet it is to be loved by you," sings James Taylor. "I want to stop, and thank you." That is what I like to do: stop and thank my Creator for filling my heart with love. Indeed, how sweet it is!

T.E.A.R.S.

True Emotions Always Release Senses

Sometimes I cry when I am happy. I let my tears flow when something sweet or beautiful touches my heart. I feel comfortable expressing my emotions. I feel them and let them go. I do not let them rule my life.

T.E.M.P.L.E.

Truth Embodied Manifests Pure
Loving Environment

One day, I ran to a temple to find solace. When I arrived,
I suddenly heard within myself, "Where my Spirit resides
is my temple." I knew in that moment I never had to
look outside of my heart to find guidance and comfort.
My heart is a temple of the Holy Spirit. Hallelujah!

T.I.G.H.T.

To Impede Glorious
Harmonious Transmissions

I love to meditate often. I relax my body to feel the sweet love flowing through my heart. I impede the harmonious flow of Consciousness if I am unfocused or uptight.

T.R.A.I.L.B.L.A.Z.E.R.

**Trust Resonance As It Lovingly Brings Light
And Zest Enabling Resourcefulness**

Resonating in Love's presence lights the way. I feel
zestful and empowered to accomplish my goals. My
resourcefulness supports me in every way. Trust me!

T.R.A.N.Q.U.I.L.

**Trust, Relax, And Now Quit
Undermining Infinite Love**

I quit undermining infinite reality when I learned
to trust, relax, and flow with what is happening in
the moment. I am able to make better choices when
I am relaxed. I breathe deeply and let go of fear and
worry. Having a peaceful presence is a gift to all.

T.R.A.N.S.M.I.T.T.E.R.

**To Receive And Now Send Meaningful
Infinite Truth To Everyone Receptive**

Serving Infinite Intelligence is the highest calling.
I share the truth conveyed to me with those
who are open to receive it. I am not attached to
whether or not what I share is acted upon.

T.R.E.A.S.U.R.E.

True Riches Endure and Supply
Unlimited Rewards Endlessly

Material riches have never motivated me. Making a
vision board did not appeal to me. My intention is
to manifest the riches that last forever. A wealth of
wisdom and love is what I desire. What I really want is to
transcend duality and live continuously in Love's light.

T.R.U.E.

To Realize Unending Existence

I do what is true for me. It is none of my business what anyone else chooses to do. Each soul has their own journey. They get to decide the path they want to take. I respect the part everyone is playing. Labeling them as "good" or "bad" only separates me from the unconditional love that I am.

T.R.U.E. G.R.I.T.

**Truth Reveals Unified Existence—Greatness
Requires Instinctive Tenacity**

I am part of everything that exists. It comforts me to know
that highly evolved beings are helping me play my part.
My responsibility is to ask for their guidance. Then I am
persistent while meeting challenges with courage and
acceptance. It takes true grit to be a spiritual warrior.

T.R.U.S.T. #1

To Realize Unlimited Self-Truth

Being a spiritual warrior takes unwavering trust. I am continuously challenged. I am guided, loved, and protected every step of the way. That increases my trust.

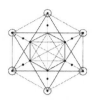

T.R.U.S.T. #2

To Receive Universal Support Today

The guidance I receive comes from Source
energy. I feel secure no matter what. My life is
harmonious and joyful. I strengthen my trust
muscle by facing my challenges with gusto.

T.R.U.S.T. #3

Try Releasing Unnecessary Stress Today

I am not deceived by the false narrative of those trying to control humanity. I know everyone and everything is evolving to a higher consciousness. All existence comes from love and is returning to love. Feeling separated from the truth is hellacious.

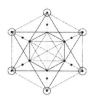

T.R.U.T.H.

To Really Understand The Heart

There is no greater knowledge than realizing that
my heart knows the truth. This one truth frees
me to be unapologetically myself. I know my
heart is leading me to ultimate freedom.

T.U.M.O.R.

To Unconsciously Manifest One's Resistance

I had breast cancer. It was the result of my false beliefs
and unconscious resistance to my sacred self. I became
more aware of my thoughts and choices. I was healed
miraculously without chemotherapy or radiation. I
trusted the guidance I received from Source when
I asked for help. The body naturally heals itself.

U.N.D.I.S.M.A.Y.E.D.

**Using Natural Discernment In Selecting Mind's
Attention Yields Enlightened Decisions**

I attract what I think about. Paying attention to
my thoughts and imagining what I want allows me
to make powerful decisions. It serves me to focus
on thoughts that result in rewarding results.

U.N.I.T.E.D.

Unity Naturally Is True Energetic Diversity

Everything is energy. Energy is boundless and eternal.
It is a fact that everything is united. Diversity is what
makes life interesting. Old creations pass, new creations
are born. It is the nature of existence. When I flow with
detachment, life becomes a celebration of its diversity.

U.P.

Unlimited Possibilities

People make vision boards to attract what they want. What I want is beyond my imagination. I am always looking past any limits! That way I attract what is best for my evolution.

V.E.S.S.E.L.

Valuable Enlightened Soul Sharing Eternal Love

I am a vessel of unconditional love sharing wisdom.
Receiving revelations from my inner guidance keeps me
present and inspired. Nothing in the material world fulfills
me more than being an instrument of divine knowledge.

V.I.B.R.A.T.I.O.N.

**Victoriously Invoking Blissful Resonance
And Tuning Into Omnipresence Now**

When I want to be in an instant, peaceful, loving
state of mind I repeat this Acrownym. This wisdom
came to me when I was distressed, but wanted to be
positive and helpful. I meditated and asked for help. I
transcended my circumstances and was filled with bliss.
I was able to proceed with kindness and compassion.

V.I.C.T.O.R.Y.

Viscerally It's Connecting To Our Real Yearning

My deepest yearning is to be all I can be without getting
in my own way. I am all I can be in the moment when I
am present and let my heart lead. Realizing this means my
life is a victorious experience now, and now, and now.

V.I.S.I.O.N.

Very Intuitive Sight Is Only Natural

Clairvoyance is natural. Daily focus and meditation increases my clairvoyant abilities. My insights inspire me into higher frequencies where magical visions appear. Every day there is a new canvas for creating the masterpiece of who I want to be.

V.I.T.A.L.

Virtuous Inner Truth And Love

I am closest to my highest Self when I am being authentic.
I express my inner truth confidently and with enthusiasm.
My childlike innocence keeps me curious, youthful, full
of wonder, and dynamic. I vitally engage with life.

V.O.I.C.E.

Vitality Offers Influential Contagious Enthusiasm

My inner child was mute. She felt unwanted. Speaking
to others was painful, especially in public. I asked her,
"What do you need?" "I want you to love me," she
whispered. I overcame my fear of speaking when I nurtured
and accepted myself as I am. Now I am one with my
younger self. Our enthusiasm is infectious, and vocal.

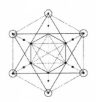

W.A.I.T.

Witness And Inwardly Trust

Witnessing my thoughts and trusting my intuition
makes it easy to wait for the fulfillment of my dreams.
I wait for the right timing. I wait for guidance to
show me my next step. I wait for the unlimited
opportunity that is making its way to me right now.

W.A.K.E. U.P.

**Wisdom And Knowing Elevates
Unlocking Potential**

When I practice shifting my awareness from fear
to love, my heart opens to receive more wisdom.
Wisdom elevates my consciousness. The more I trust
and know myself, the more opportunities arise.

W.A.R.R.I.O.R.

**Wisdom And Right Responses Impacts
One's Resonance**

Being aligned with Truth allows me to respond
powerfully. Resonating with Higher Consciousness
impacts everyone and everything. I am a love warrior.

W.A.Y.

With Awareness Yielding

Yielding to the wisdom of Higher Consciousness literally makes life an exciting adventure. Yes, there are challenges—that is part of life. But knowing my next step is always guided is the perfect way to relax and enjoy playing my part. I am the way the truth and the life.

W.E.A.L.T.H.

With Enthusiasm And Light Treasures Happen

Acting with enthusiasm attracts treasures beyond
measure. The Light of Consciousness is the truest
wealth. Without it, there is nothing worthwhile.
With it, there is everything priceless and eternal.

W.E.A.L.T.H.Y.

Wisdom Enlightens And Love Truly Heals You

Having wealth without joy is not being wealthy.
Having a healthy attitude is a treasure money cannot
buy. Love heals all wounds. Love is abundantly
available to anyone who opens to receive it. I am
the wealthiest person I know. What I need is always
provided. And what I desire is on its way to me now.

W.E.L.C.O.M.E.

**When Everyone Lovingly Caresses
Others Miracles Ensue**

Since everyone is an expression of the One Self, welcoming others is welcoming myself. *Namaste* is a salutation that means, "I bow to the divine in you which is the divine me." Loving everyone on the human level may not be possible. It is possible to love everyone's divine spirit.

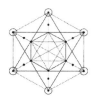

W.E.L.L.B.E.I.N.G.

**With Enthusiasm Loving Light Brings
Inner Natural Greatness**

There is nothing greater than knowing oneself. My
purpose is to share my gifts, my natural talents, which
help to inspire and uplift humanity. My wellbeing
does not depend on anything outside of myself.

W.H.A.T.

Who Has A Thought?

My mind has thoughts continuously. My soul determines
which thoughts to act on and which thoughts to watch
with detachment. Peace and power come from being the
commander of my thoughts, not the slave to them.

W.H.E.N.

We Have Everything Now

In a split second, I could lose every material thing
I have. It happens to many every day. All I need is
within me and can never be lost. Even if I die, my
spirit goes on in the natural creative flow of the
universe. I have everything that matters now.

W.H.E.R.E.

Wise Hearts Expand Reaching Everywhere

I expand beyond my physical limits when I
meditate. I am one with all life and exist everywhere.
That is where I enjoy visiting frequently.

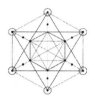

W.H.O.L.E.

With Hearts Open Love Expresses

Being whole is knowing I am pure Love. I come from
Love. I express Love. I return to Love! Love is all there is.

W.H.Y.

Wisdom Heals You

I have been on a self-realization journey for as long as I can remember. Why do I seek the truth? Each new nugget of wisdom sets a part of me free. My journey will never end. I will simply merge with the vibration of eternal truth.

W.I.N.

Wholeness Is Natural

I won the game of life when I realized I am
whole and complete, exactly as I am. I always
have been and always will be. End of story.

W.I.S.D.O.M. #1

With Intention Soul Develops
Omnipotent Mindfulness

Wisdom is revealed to me when my mind is still and my
heart is open. I intend to listen to my inner self. I am
mindful of my choices, guided by Omnipotent Intelligence.

W.I.S.D.O.M. #2

Why Is Self Discovery One's Mission

My purpose is to know myself. It is the reason
for being. Love and wisdom never perish.

W.I.S.E.

With Intuition Spirit Enlightens

I am bound to act wisely when I listen to my
intuition. It is my Spirit speaking to me.

W.I.T.H.I.N.

Wisdom Is Truth Happening Inwardly Now

I know what is true when I pay attention to what my heart is telling me. All the answers to all of my questions are within me. It is my responsibility to listen and act accordingly.

W.O.N.D.E.R.F.U.L.L.Y.

**Wisely Observing Nature's Diverse Expressions
Restores Feeling Unlimited Light Lifting You**

Nature has a way of shifting my awareness from my
thoughts to my heart. I am in awe of the variety
of beauty and wonder in creation. Being in nature
lifts my spirits and is wonderfully refreshing.

W.O.N.D.R.O.U.S.L.Y.

**With Omnipotent Nature's Diverse Resources
One's Untethered Self Lovingly Yields**

My abundant Source energy gives all manner of
things to me unconditionally. I gratefully yield to
the natural gifts of nature, a cool breeze, the sweet
smells after the rain, the crickets singing me to
sleep. I am wondrously living with awe and joy.

W.O.R.D.S.

Ways Of Remembering Divine Source

Words are very powerful. They can be used to discourage or encourage. They can rob us of our potential or enhance our lives. I pay attention to the words I use. I speak words of wisdom that enlighten and inspire. I am a wordsmith.

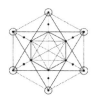

W.O.R.Y.

Wasting Own Resources Resisting Yourself

Worry is a great waste of time and resources. Worry
depletes energy and causes depression. Staying
in tune with the Infinite releases all worries. My
alignment leads me to what I need when I need it.

W.O.R.S.H.I.P.

We Offer Reverent Sincere Hearts in Praise

My heart is in praise of the Divine all throughout the day. I honor my life by being grateful for each breath I take. I give continuous thanks for being present with whatever I am doing. Thus, joy is the nature of my moment-to-moment existence.

Y.E.S.

You Expect Success

I expect unlimited opportunities to materialize
for me effortlessly. My talents are worthy of being
celebrated. I expect to be successful in my endeavors.
I say "Yes!" to life's abundant opportunities.

Y.O.G.A.

You're Offering God All

I taught yoga for years and loved it. The purpose of the *asanas* or postures is to bring us in union with our divine nature. I surrender my human self and merge with the One Self.

Z.E.S.T.

Zestfully Expressing Self Truth

Being my true self is my purpose. Being true to myself
brings me the greatest joy. My heart overflows with
gratitude as I zestfully express my authentic self.

ABOUT THE AUTHOR

JJ Crow is a spiritual seeker who has found inner peace by imbibing the wisdom from the sacred texts of spiritual masters, poets, and mystics. She continues to gain wisdom by listening to enlightened spiritual warriors raising the collective consciousness. She is the sovereign master of her own destiny.

JJ served in the U.S. Department of State Foreign Service for three two-year tours. She learned from her extensive travel in different countries that the primary desire of people everywhere was to find inner peace. She has lived in an ashram and attended spiritual retreats in America and India.

In 1991, JJ published *The I AM Cards,* a divination tool for self-realization. That same year, she experienced a spontaneous healing of breast cancer. She was shown she would receive a miracle healing, so she refused chemotherapy and radiation treatment. Recently, she used an inspired self-healing meditation that cured her of debilitating arthritis.

JJ was a certified masseuse for over forty years and has been a certified yoga teacher for over twenty-five years. She shares inspired wisdom in HolyCrow Acrownyms newsletters and teaches meditation to clients wanting to slow down, heal, and find inner peace.

JJ lives in Sonoma, California. She enjoys walking, stretching, preparing healthy meals, and daily meditations.

Learn more about JJ at www.holycrowacronyms.com.

Follow JJ on Social

Instagram: @jjcrow2

Facebook: @jj.crow.58

Made in the USA
Las Vegas, NV
12 December 2023